I0759434

Perseverance *landed on Mars in 2021 and is still active.*

AI IN THE WORLD

12 USES FOR ARTIFICIAL INTELLIGENCE IN SPACE

BLACK RABBIT BOOKS

Table of Contents

Rovers Travel Across Mars *with AI*

1

In 1997, the **rover** *Sojourner* landed on Mars. It was part of the National Aeronautics and Space Administration's (NASA) Mars Pathfinder mission. It was also the first rover on Mars.

Sojourner used artificial intelligence (AI) as it drove around the planet. If it "sensed" danger, it would move away. The next rovers, *Spirit* and *Opportunity*, landed in 2004. They had a more advanced AI. They could see objects and plan paths around them.

Mars is also known as the Red Planet.

Curiosity, which landed in 2011, used deep learning and **neural networks**. It also had computer vision. It could do research. It could choose where to go. And it could decide how safe an area was.

Perseverance arrived in 2021. Its AI was called **Autonomous** Exploration for Gathering Increased

Science (AGEIS). It could find certain minerals. It could collect data on the things it saw.

The next rover is called *Rosalind Franklin*. It is part of the European Space Agency (ESA) Mars program. Its mission is to look for signs of life on the planet. The rover will have a machine learning AI. The AI can filter through data.

Rovers have a limited amount of time in space. They can only send a few samples back to Earth. *Rosalind Franklin* will decide what is most important or interesting.

As of 2025, six rovers have been sent to Mars.

AI as the Next *Astronomer*

2

Outer space is huge. Scientists think that there could be 1 septillion stars in the universe. That's a 1 followed by 24 zeroes! Space is full of planets and moons. There are billions of galaxies and star systems. How do scientists keep track of it all?

Mapping the stars teaches scientists about space. But it is expensive to map new sections of the universe. Scientists do not always get a detailed, 3D view. Space is not just an empty area. It is dense and full of objects. They all have different masses and gravity.

Things like **dark matter** can change a galaxy's shape. It pushes and pulls stars in different directions. It affects how close or how far planets are from each other. But scientists need to know how much dark matter is in an area.

TEAMWORK MAKES DREAM WORK

Telescopes around the world map the night sky. The photos they take are full of information. AI learning software can look at billions of light dots in just one telescope image. It tells scientists which things are the most important.

Deep space travel could be possible with the help of AI.

In 2024, scientists used an AI called SimBIG. It looked at 2,000 different space **simulations**. Each had their own rules and conditions. They were based off real data and research. SimBIG took that information. It made new universes.

Scientists compared SimBIG's universes to real ones. They used data from more than 100,000 galaxies. They proved that the AI could be used to fill in the blanks.

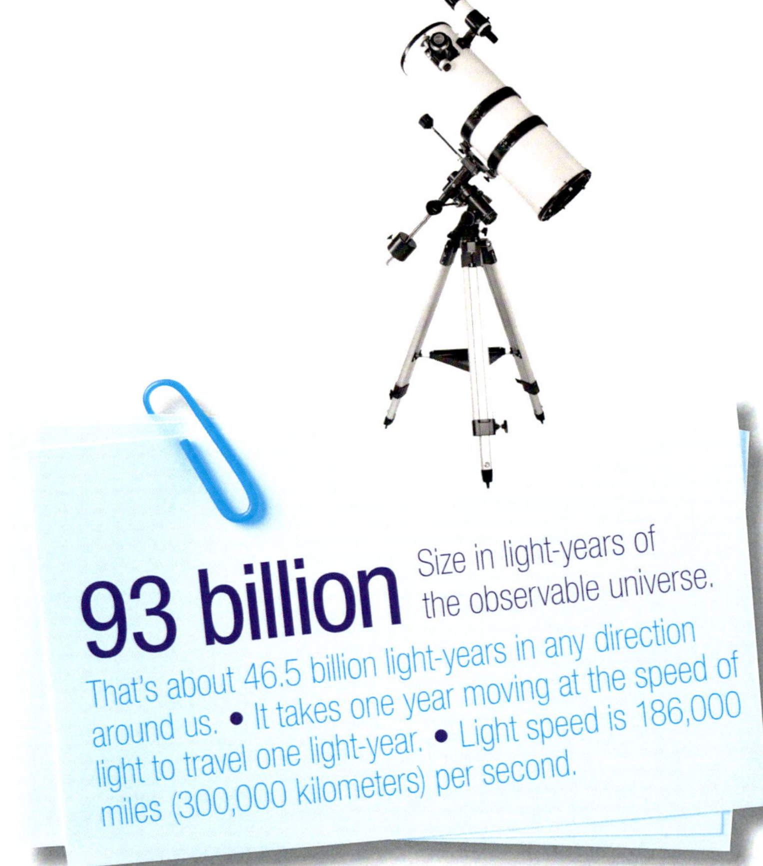

AI Speeds Up the Search for *Extraterrestrial Life*

3

Some people look at outer space as the future of human life. But others are looking for life that already exists in outer space.

The SETI Institute watches the sky for signs of **extraterrestrial** activity. SETI stands for the Search for Extraterrestrial Intelligence. SETI members are open to the idea of other intelligent beings.

Humans send signals into space all the time. Radio, TV, and radar signals could let alien life know we exist. And those same aliens could be sending their own signals out toward us.

SETI scans the sky. It looks for radio signals from space. So far, scientists have looked at more than 1,000 star systems. They use software to filter signals. They sort which ones came from Earth. There is a lot of information to look at. It takes a long time.

Nvidia's Holoscan processes those signals faster. It works with an AI program called IGX. IGX and Holoscan work together to find signals in real time. When humans and regular computers get them, they can't look at every signal. They might have to skip some of them. There is not enough time to look at every single one. But IGX can. It looks at every signal and returns results twice as fast as a human.

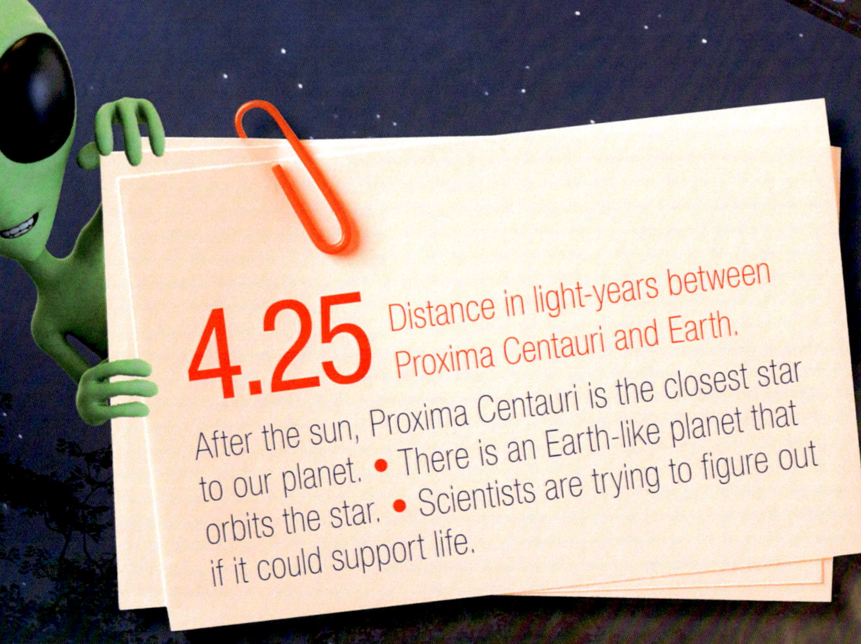

Think About It

Do you believe in aliens? Why or why not? Back up your opinion with three facts.

Movies often show alien ships kidnapping people—and sometimes animals.

NASA Uses Unreal Engine to Simulate *Life on Mars*

4

Unreal Engine is a game engine. It has been used to build video games such as *Fortnite*, *Rocket League*, and *Gears of War*. It can make high-quality graphics. It creates realistic simulations. NASA has been partnered with Unreal Engine since 2016. Their goal? To prepare astronauts for Mars.

The NASA XR Operations Support System (XOSS) works with virtual reality (VR). They use physics engines and sensors. They try out custom software. With VR's help, XOSS makes worlds that look real. It can copy conditions on the Moon and Mars. Astronauts can train in real-time.

XOSS has been building a **metaverse** using Unreal Engine's built-in AI. It is available to anyone 18 or older. It has tools that lets people design and create their own educational tests or games.

5 Number of challenge categories in the MarsXR Challenge.

Four categories challenged inventors to improve on NASA technology. • The fifth category was Blow Our Minds. It was awarded for never-before-seen creativity and innovation. • The top 20 ideas shared a prize of $70,000.

AI simulations can help astronauts learn how to live on Mars.

In 2023, NASA began the MarsXR Challenge. It asked developers to come up with new simulations or equipment. There were prizes for the winners.

One winner of the challenge was Trillium Technologies. They created an AI glider. It would be able to find fossilized life on the surface of Mars. It used machine learning to identify **biosignatures**. A glider could cover areas hundreds of miles wide. Viewers could control the glider from a tablet. They could also get a third-person view from the air.

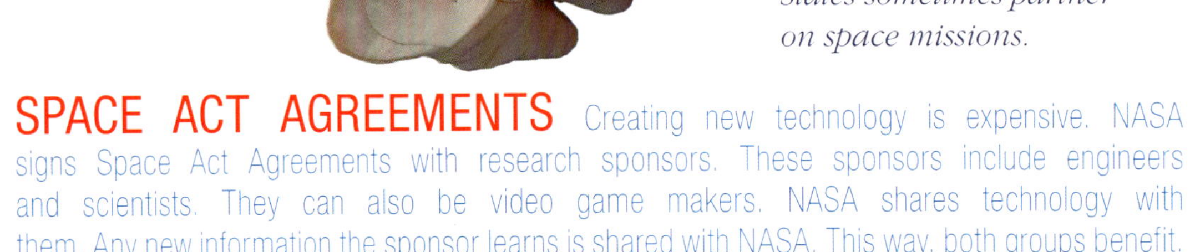

Russia and the United States sometimes partner on space missions.

SPACE ACT AGREEMENTS Creating new technology is expensive. NASA signs Space Act Agreements with research sponsors. These sponsors include engineers and scientists. They can also be video game makers. NASA shares technology with them. Any new information the sponsor learns is shared with NASA. This way, both groups benefit.

AI Helps Steer Around *Space Debris*

5

Humans started exploring space in 1957. By 2025, about 6,840 rockets had been launched. Around 20,650 **satellites** have been sent into orbit around Earth. They are used for navigation and communication. Others look at Earth or outer space. However, only about half of them still work today.

Some satellites have fuel left before they die. They are moved to fall out of orbit. They burn up as they reenter Earth's atmosphere. But others just stop working. They become trash. Sometimes they hit each other. Each time two objects crash into each other, pieces break off. The broken pieces can fly off and hit other objects. There are now millions of pieces of **debris** floating around in space.

Today, the amount of space debris is dangerous. It moves fast. The US Air Force tracks all objects in space that are larger than a softball. That's around 30,000 pieces! But there are millions of pieces that are smaller than 0.04 inches (1 millimeter). AI can keep track of these tiny but dangerous bits.

You-Only-Look-Once (YOLO) is deep learning AI. It looks at a picture and finds objects in it. It has been used to track space debris. It has proven to be faster and more accurate than any radar systems used before.

14,872 Weight in tons (13,500 metric tons) of all space objects in Earth's orbit.

Space debris moves 10 times faster than a bullet. • Between 1999 and 2023, the International Space Station had to adjust course 32 times. • It moved to avoid satellites and space debris.

Earth's upper atmosphere is full of space debris.

Self-driving cars use AI to move without a driver.

6

Self-Docking Spaceships Aid *in Efficiency*

Self-driving cars are the future on Earth. They use AI. AI keeps them on the road. It helps them dodge things in their way. The cars make their own decisions. They can keep passengers safe. Stanford's Autonomous Systems Lab has been working on self-driving cars. They are also using that tech for space travel.

The same AI used in self-driving cars may help spacecraft dock.

Many people work with the Center for Aerospace Autonomy Research (CAESAR). Stanford University is one partner. Other colleges and government groups are involved too. Their first goal is to help spacecraft dock safely.

Teaching a car to park itself can be tricky. Sensors tell the car how much to turn or back up. They look at things that don't move. They use those things as guides. Parking a shuttle in space is harder. Stars could be used as guides. But things in space are always moving. AI would need to locate stars again to line up with them properly.

Using AI could make docking smoother and faster. It could make split-second decisions. Then it could adjust as needed. CAESAR's AI is called the Autonomous Rendezvous Transformer (ART). ART would look at past dockings. It would plan the best way to line up the shuttle. Then it would make sure its plan met safety rules. ART could save both time and fuel.

AI will make docking at the ISS much easier.

AI Gives a Hand to *the ISS*

7

The International Space Station (ISS) circles Earth 16 times a day. It travels at speeds of 17,900 miles (28,807 km) per hour. It is expensive to care for. But it's also important. It teaches scientists about outer space.

The ISS already has two robotic arms. One is Canada's Canadarm2. The other is Japan's Experiment Module Remote Manipulator. The arms can move supplies. They help space vehicles land. They can do repairs to the ISS. Both arms are controlled by astronauts. Being able to do things outside without leaving the ISS keeps astronauts safe.

The ESA's European Robotic Arm (ERA) is the future of robotic tools. It has an elbow and shoulders. It also has wrists. The arm can "walk" around the ISS. People can control it from inside and outside. But it can also make its own choices.

Think About It

What would you do if you had a robot assistant? How would it make your life easier?

Using the AI-powered robotic arms helps keep astronauts safe.

A similar piece of technology is being built to go to Mars. The ESA's Sample Transfer Arm will pick up tubes left by *Perseverance*. It will place the tubes in a container. Then it will seal the container and fly away. Using AI, it will decide what to do next. The containers will be part of the Mars Sample Return mission. That mission is planned to take place in 2030.

37 Length in feet (11.3 meters) that ERA can stretch.

It has seven joints. Both ends of the arm can act as a hand. • It also has four cameras and lights. • ERA assists the Russian section of the ISS.

AI Solves Problems in *Advance*

8

In 1970, the Apollo 13 spacecraft exploded. It was trying to get back to Earth. After the accident, NASA began exploring "digital twins." A digital twin is like a computer copy of a real spaceship. The twins help scientists find and fix problems before they happen.

The *James Webb Space Telescope* launched in late 2021. It is one of the biggest and most powerful telescopes to date. Its mission is very important. A digital twin helped make sure the mission was a success.

One side of the telescope faces the Sun. It gets very hot. The other side faces away and gets very cold. The telescope has two main parts. One is its core. The other is its sunshield. This protects the tools on board.

The core is about two stories tall and two stories wide. The sunshield folded out after the telescope reached its resting place. When open, the sunshield is the size of a tennis court. Both were too big to test on Earth. Both have digital twins.

The virtual models used generative AI. They showed NASA hundreds of ways the telescope might fail. The engineers planned for each one. *Webb* reached its spot in space on January 24, 2022. Because of the tests, everything went perfectly.

The James Webb Space Telescope *is about 1 million miles (1.6 million km) from Earth.*

$10 billion Amount it cost to build the Webb telescope.

Webb orbits the Sun. It is 1 million miles (1.6 million kilometers) away from Earth. • Webb's first photos were released in July 2022. • It has discovered galaxies that are far away. It has also found new stars and planets.

You are here.

The Webb telescope has taken pictures of faraway galaxies.

AI Robots Could Set Up *Camp in Space*

9 If you left today, you could touch down on Mars in seven to nine months. You would have to bring everything you needed in one trip. Running out of supplies would not be an option.

Robots do not need food or water. They can harvest resources such as water or oxygen. They can store them so people can use them later.

Machine learning robots will be able to that. They could set up camp before people arrive. The robots would find the best places to explore. They could map out new areas. They could keep older equipment running. And they could send back information on the planet's conditions. All of this would help astronauts plan ahead.

In 2023, an AI "chemist" used machine learning. It learned from meteorites from Mars. It also looked at

Rovers like Perseverance *can pave the way for human life on Mars.*

space rocks. These rocks are made up of different elements and minerals than rocks on Earth.

There were more than 3.7 million ways elements from the space rocks could be broken down to make oxygen. It would take a person 2,000 years to figure out the best combinations. The AI chemist did it in a few weeks.

SELF-REPLICATING AI In 2025, researchers tried something new. They asked two AI programs to make copies of themselves. One AI succeeded 50 percent of the time. The other succeeded 90 percent of the time. Some people worry that AI might one day become self-aware and work against people. This is called rogue AI. Learning about AI now could help stop that from happening.

An artist's concept drawing of a base on Mars.

Astrobees Help with *Common Tasks*

10 Sci-fi TV shows and movies often show humans working with robots. The robots may be maids or mechanics. They might be used as soldiers. Sometimes, they are friends or helpers. But they are always there to make a human's life easier.

In 2018 and 2019, NASA built three cube-shaped robots to make astronauts' lives easier. They were part of the Astrobee program. The Astrobees use fans to move through **microgravity**. Cameras help them see where they are going. Each has an arm to grab handrails or objects. When they need a charge, they return to their docking stations.

Astrobees save astronauts time every day. They are fully autonomous. They can solve problems on their own. They can explore and map out new areas. They can

12.5 Width in inches (32 centimeters) of an Astrobee robot.

The robots are named Honey, Bumble, and Queen. • By 2025, they had helped with more than 150 different tasks. • Hundreds of students have sent new **code** to the ISS for the Astrobees.

AI-powered Astrobees move through the ISS to help with research.

track supplies and record experiments. A human can also control the Astrobees.

Interchangeable arms let the Astrobees help in different ways. They can hold objects. They can grab things out of the air. Tentacle-like arms have sticky pads at the end. They are like frog or lizard feet.

Someday, Astrobees could do space walks. They could hold onto satellites. Then they could fix them or replace parts. They could even refuel them.

The Astrobee's soft arm sticks to surfaces like a frog's foot.

ADDING TO THE ASTROBEE Students from around the world can play with the Astrobees. The Kibo Robot Programming Challenge encourages students to write code for them. Winners get to see the robots test out their programs.

11

AI Companions Keep Astronauts *Company in Space*

Mars missions will last nearly three years. Being lonely would be a big problem. Astronauts on the ISS can talk to people back on Earth. But there can be a several-second delay. On Mars, that delay could be as long as 24 minutes. Having conversations would be hard.

AI chatbots on Earth are already being used to keep people company. They use conversational AI to copy human speech. Natural language processing helps the AI understand what a human is saying. It helps them figure out what to say back. There are bots that type and some that speak.

Henry the Helper is a robot. He was made by NASA's Jet Propulsion Laboratory. Henry can talk to people. He can help them do tests. Henry has deep learning AI. Every time Henry chats, he learns more about human emotion.

Future space machines will have something like ChatGPT. Before, astronauts had to look through guides and manuals. They needed instructions on how to communicate with rovers and satellites. But chat features will let them actually talk to the machines. This would make tasks faster and easier. It could also give astronauts the sense of speaking with a friend.

Frank Rubio

A LONG, LONG TRIP In March 2025, astronauts Suni Williams and Butch Wilmore returned to Earth. They had been on the ISS for 286 days. Technical issues kept them from coming back. But they do not hold the record for the longest ISS visitors. That belongs to Frank Rubio. He was there for 371 days!

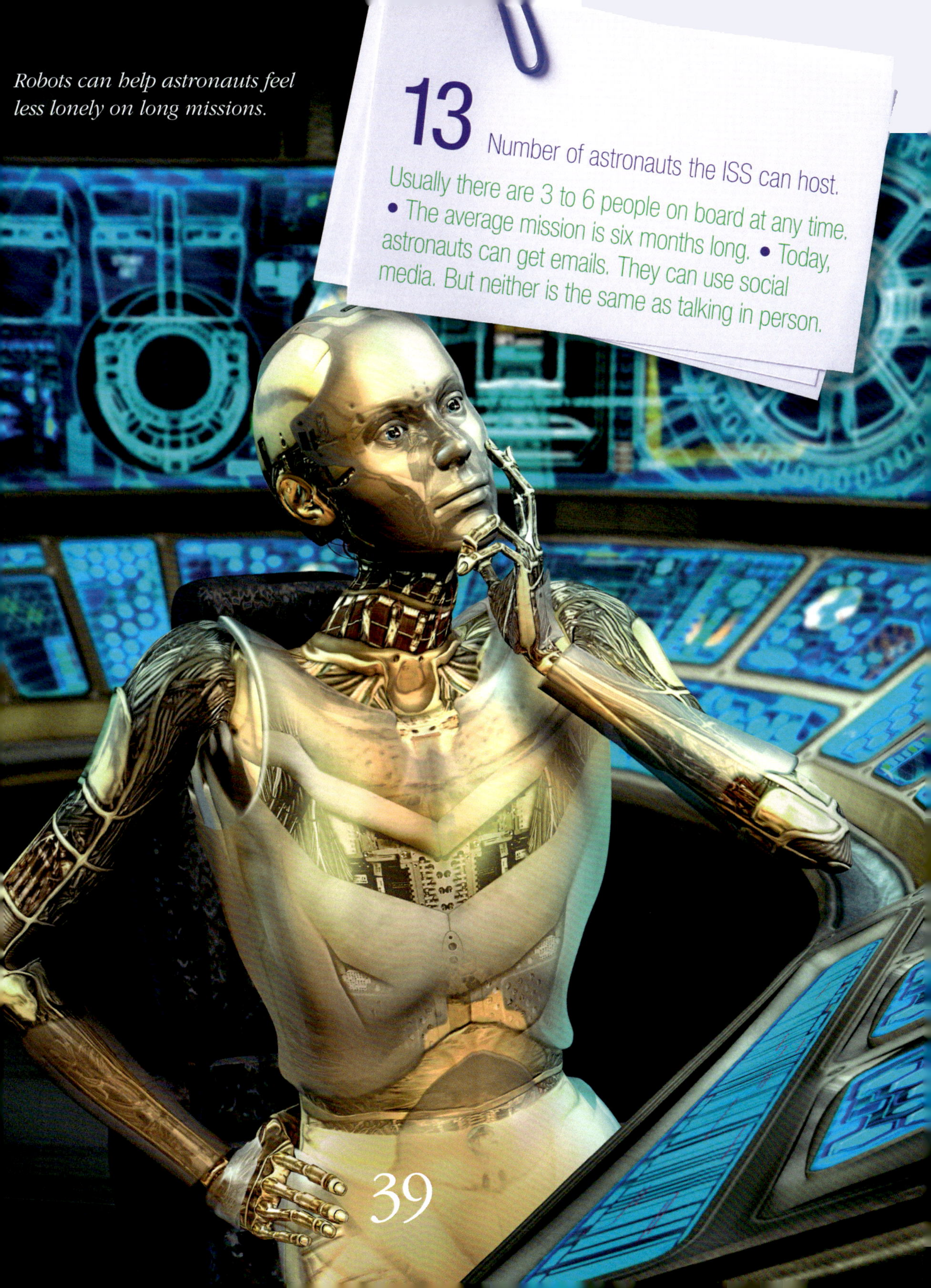

Robots can help astronauts feel less lonely on long missions.

13 Number of astronauts the ISS can host.

Usually there are 3 to 6 people on board at any time. • The average mission is six months long. • Today, astronauts can get emails. They can use social media. But neither is the same as talking in person.

AI Can Help in Space *Emergencies*

12

Accidents can happen anywhere. On Earth, people can call 911. But in space, astronauts are on their own. NASA has a health and medical officer on Earth. There are also special doctors called flight surgeons. Each mission has its own. They meet with astronauts once a week.

Astronauts might go into space with basic medical knowledge. But for emergencies, they are on their own. They have limited supplies. Communication with the flight surgeon could be slow. AI could provide support when needed.

NASA is exploring AI systems that would be equipped with medical information and tools. These systems would use large language AI models that can respond to human voices. The AI would have access to astronauts' medical records and data from previous missions. It could test out “what if” situations that might come up during long missions. Plans could be made before a problem even happens.

Once in space, the AI could check things like heart rate and body temperature. It could suggest changes to help with health and wellness. It might also recommend medicine if needed. AI could even guide astronauts through certain things like giving stitches.

Sick astronauts have choices in a medical emergency.

14 Number of days before life in space begins affecting the human body.
Astronauts lose both bone density and muscle mass. • The muscles that help people stand up are affected first. • Astronauts in space exercise for around 2.5 hours every day. However, this is still not enough to stop negative effects on the body.

Think About It

Would you rather have a human or AI as a doctor? Why?

AI helps doctors save lives both on Earth and in space!

Fact

- AI-powered satellites are used to watch Earth. The ESA has one called Φsat-2 (phi-sat-two). It launched in 2024. It can turn images into maps. It can track clouds and warn about bad weather. It can see changes in the ocean. It can sense wildfires. Its AI decides which images are the most important. It makes the image files smaller before it sends them back to Earth. This saves on download time.
- The photos taken by the *James Webb Space Telescope* look amazing. But they do not look like that straight from the telescope. There are a lot of things in the sky. AI is being used to clean up the pictures. It can unblur images. It turns them into clear pictures that are easier to understand.

Sheet

• Dark matter and dark energy make up more than 95 percent of all energy in the universe. But scientists still don't know much about either. They use AI to look for patterns in galaxies. Scientists hope that someday they can track changes by looking at dark matter and energy.

• Astronauts and scientists are using AI to look at space. But regular astronomers can test it out too. Smart telescopes can make it easy for beginners to get started. AI-powered software tells users what they are seeing. It makes what they see clearer. It can even follow objects in the sky.

Glossary

autonomous
Something that can function and complete tasks without being controlled by a human.

biosignature
A special clue or fingerprint that tells us something lived there, such as a fossil.

code
Instructions for a computer program.

dark matter
A mysterious substance that affects and shapes things in space.

debris
Scattered waste or remains.

extraterrestrial
Coming from or existing outside the earth or its atmosphere.

metaverse
A virtual space where users can interact with the environment and other users.

microgravity
When things seem to be weightless.

neural network
A super smart computer program inspired by the human brain.

rover
A vehicle used for exploring the surface of a planet or other space body.

satellite
A machine sent into space that moves around a planet, star, or moon.

simulation
Something that is made to look, feel, or behave like something real.

For More Information

Books

Bolte, Mari. *Mysteries Revealed.* Ann Arbor, Mich.: Cherry Lake Press, 2023.

Hubbard, Ben. *NASA's Artemis Missions: Exploring the Moons.* Minneapolis: Lerner Publications.

Websites

Mars Exploration Rover Facts for Kids
kids.kiddle.co/Mars_Exploration_Rover

NASA Science Space Place
spaceplace.nasa.gov/menu/play/webb/

About the Author

Mari Bolte is a writer and editor who enjoys wondering about where the future of technology will take us. Whether it's exploring outer space or thinking about how AI can make her life easier, one might say she has her head in "the cloud."

Index

TOP RANK is published by Black Rabbit Books, P.O. Box 227, Mankato, MN, 56002.

• Edited by Ana Brauer • Designed by Danny Nanos • Photographs © Dreamstime/Ahmad Bayrakdar, 7, Tranz2d, 12; Getty Images/Caspar Benson, 16, William Whitehurst, 39; NASA/unknown, 26, 35; Shutterstock/Alena Brozova, 40, Andrei Armiagov, 44, Anterovium, 4, Belinda Pretorius, 48, buradaki, 2–3, 8, 45, Dabarti CGI, 19, Denis Belitsky, 9, Denis---S, 12–13, Dima Zel, 27, Elnur, 42–43, FotograFFF, 21, Frame Stock Footage, 14, frantic00, 6, Istvan Hajas, 17, Jolygon, 46–47, metamorworks, 20–21, NicoElNino, 37, Paopano, 25, paulista, 32–33, photoHare, 2, 10, 45, Sergey Nivens, 15, servickuz, cover, 1, Stockbym, 5, Thaiview, 11, Triff, 30–31, vovan, 41, xpixel, 34, 36, 24K-Production, 28, 29, 44, 3Dsculptor, 22–23; Wikimedia Commons/NASA/Frank Rubio, 38 • Printed in the United States of America.

Library of Congress Cataloging-in-Publication Data: Names: Bolte, Mari author | Title: 12 uses for artificial intelligence in space / by Mari Bolte. | Other titles: Twelve uses for artificial intelligence in space | Description: Mankato, MN: Black Rabbit Books, [2026] | Series: AI in the world | Includes bibliographical references and index. | Audience: Ages 9–13 | Audience: Grades 4–6 | Identifiers: LCCN 2025021458 (print) | LCCN 2025021459 (ebook) | ISBN 9781645825180 library binding | ISBN 9781645825364 paperback | ISBN 9781645825548 ebook | Subjects: LCSH: Astronautics—Data processing—Juvenile literature | Artificial intelligence—Technological innovations—Juvenile literature | Outer space—Exploration—Technological innovations—Juvenile literature | Classification: LCC TL793 .B624 2026 (print) | LCC TL793 (ebook) | LC record available at https://lccn.loc.gov/2025021458 | LC ebook record available at https://lccn.loc.gov/2025021459